Oil Ventures 101 is a trademark of Robert Wellesley. Copyright 2012. All rights reserved. No part of this book may be used or reproduced in any manner whatsoever without written permission except in the case of brief quotations embodied in critical articles and reviews. For information, contact the author through the address below.

FIRST EDITION published November 2012

Published by Sequence Publishing
Austin, Texas

www.OilVentures1O1.org

to contact the author for any reason, please send an email to:
• **OilVentures101@gmail.com**

Additional contact information at end of book

This book is intended for informational purposes only. It is not intended to replace the advice or counseling of an investment professional.

Information found throughout this entire book is not an offer to buy nor sell a security or any investment, nor is this a general solicitation of any sort. An offer to sell a security may only be made by a private placement memorandum to accredited investors where permitted by law. The purpose of this book is merely for general informational and research purposes.

This book is not intended to be the final authority on this topic, but merely to educate the reader. While the book strives to be as timely, detailed, concise, and complete as possible, neither the author nor Oil Ventures 101 guarantees nor asserts that this book is free of errors or omissions, nor that the information contained herein is the most recent available. Furthermore, local laws with regard to oil investing do vary, depending on the jurisdiction.

Thus, prior to engaging in any oil investing, the reader is strongly advised to consult with a seasoned investment professional, one with expertise in oil ventures, who will be able to procure the latest information relevant to your situation as well as providing other consultancy services.

Table of Contents

PREFACE: OIL VENTURES -- THE SAGE INVESTMENT..........7
INTRODUCTION – WHO INVESTS IN OIL VENTURES?..........9
   The Dependable and Lucrative Investment..........10
   A Wealth Generating Commodity..........11
   Domestic Oil Drilling Companies..........12
   Exploratory vs Developmental Drilling..........13
   The Revolution in Exploration..........14
   Types of Partnerships..........14
   Investor Requirements..........15
   Minimizing Risks..........16

1: WHY OIL IS SUCH A VITAL COMMODITY..........17
   Competing Energy Technologies..........20
      Nuclear Fission..........20
      Coal..........20
      Biofuels..........20
      Solar..........21
      Wind..........21
      Geothermal..........22
      Water Power..........22
      Nuclear Fusion..........22
      Other, more esoteric technologies..........22

2: SUMMARY OF DOMESTIC OIL INDUSTRY..........25
   Exploratory vs Developmental Drilling..........26
      Drilling Procedures..........27
      Advances in Exploration Technology..........28
   Types Of Ownership..........28
      Accredited Investor..........29

3: OIL VENTURES – BENEFITS AND REWARDS..........31
   Quick Initial Payback..........32
   Long Term Value..........32
   Big Upside Potential..........32

Established, Liquid Market..32
Stable & Safe Investment..33
Protected Asset...33
Increasing Market Demand Coupled With Decreasing Supply......33
Decreasing Risk Profile..34
Lucrative..34
Considerable Tax Benefits..34
Tax Breaks In Detail 36
   Depreciation..36
   Tangible completion expenses...36
   Depletion allowance..36
   Geological deductions...36
   Self-employment tax/conversion from general to limited partner...37
   Alternative minimum tax...37
   Passive activity exception..37
   Special rule for timing of deductions...............................37
   Marginal well production credits.....................................38

4: OIL VENTURES – RISKS AND HOW TO AVOID THEM.......39
Risk: Dry Hole..40
   How To Minimize The Risk Of Dry Holes........................40
Risk: Bad Companies..40
   Inexperienced Drilling Companies..................................40
   Unscrupulous Companies..40
   Scam Artists...41
Not Getting Involved With Inexperienced Or Scam Companies....43
Conclusion..51

Etc...53
Consult With Legitimate Oil Venture Firms...................................53
ABOUT the Author..54
ABOUT OilVentures101.org..54

Preface: Oil ventures -- the sage investment

OIL VENTURES 101

We all know the obvious – that oil literally makes the modern world work. An industry worth $35,000,000,000,000 (35 trillion dollars) oil and gas development is the single biggest business sector on the globe. Many very smart people constantly invest and re-invest enormous sums of money into oil precisely because it is such a lucrative investment.

While you might make a few dollars investing in oil company stocks, mutual funds, ETFs, commodities or futures, the big money is in 'oil ventures' - direct investment in developmental oil and gas drilling - provided you have a good, fundamental understanding of the risks and that you have funds adequate to legally qualify as an investor.

The oil and gas ventures industry is so vital to our modern way of life that the U.S. government has long offered extraordinary and unique tax breaks and benefits that are solely available to individuals and companies investing in the oil and gas sector.

Given a detailed review of the information on the following pages, you will have become considerably better informed regarding the immense and numerous benefits, as well as the potential risk of committing your hard-earned money to this most sage of investments.

OIL VENTURES 101

INTRODUCTION – WHO INVESTS IN OIL VENTURES?

Oil drilling is a very old and stable form of investment. This may seem to be a surprising statement, given that far too often one hears of investors getting snagged into scams or losing their investments in a series of dry wells. But the reality is that these stories are outliers – the extreme cases in a vast industry with many levels of entry and many levels of risk.

The Dependable and Lucrative Investment

Given that the potential investor is armed with the right information - a good, fundamental knowledge of potential pitfalls, funds adequate to mitigate any setbacks, and the will to do proper due diligence work on the specifics of a deal - there is no reason the typical oil venture investor cannot enjoy consistent annual returns of 50% for decades, along with the tremendous income tax benefits that the U.S. grants exclusively to oil and gas venture investors. As with any investment, it is quite possible to lose some or all of one's investment, but with the right project or portfolio of projects, it is also not uncommon for the small investor to see a 5:1 or even a 10:1 return on their initial investment. Few investment vehicles today offer such promising returns.

There is a reason the U.S. Government has employed a slew of lucrative tax benefits that are exclusive to the oil ventures industry - oil and gas is absolutely critical to our modern way of life. Despite talk of new energy sources and technologies eventually displacing oil, the truth is that oil is a keystone energy source – relatively easy and inexpensive to acquire, process, transport, and use, with a high energy output per given amount of fuel, and an extensive, built out infrastructure.

As a result of oil's usefulness, oil consumption continues to skyrocket, with global demand doubling roughly every decade. This demand for oil is reflected in the stock market – whereas stocks have been nearly flat this past decade, oil and gas prices are up more than 300% since 2000, with some experts predicting a 400% increase in prices during this current decade.

The U.S. Government also strongly encourages domestic oil production in order to reduce our nation's dependence on foreign oil. Domestic oil stockpiles are at a nearly 30 year low, with oil imports at over 60%, double what they were prior to the U.S. oil embargo.

Lucrative returns and extraordinary tax incentives have long attracted investors to oil and gas. Profits can be enormous and royalty checks can come for decades. The tax benefits alone are such that many investors have their initial investment return back to them in as little as 6 to 18 months. What is unprecedented about these tax breaks and write-offs is that a high income bracket oil investor, had they not invested the money into oil in the first place, would have just seen the money be sent off to the U.S. government in the form of income taxes anyway. Additionally, using other tax breaks, investors can generally write off nearly the entire oil investment, regardless of whether the oil well turns up dry or not.

A Wealth Generating Commodity

Oil is how many of the wealthiest people on earth became so wealthy. The range of oil industry investor types today includes not just wealthy individuals, but foreign investors, trust departments of major banks, large life insurance companies, major industrial companies, and pension funds that invest in oil and gas drilling strictly for profit, as they have no need for the tax benefits.

Domestically, the U.S. oil industry further relies on a smaller scale eco-system of small-to-midsize oil drilling companies, generally family run operations that have been in business successfully for decades. These drilling companies rely on a network of private investors, many of whom make their initial foray into oil investing as little as $25k or $50k. The reason these smaller companies are so vital is that the majors, the Exxons and Chevrons, have largely transitioned their operations offshore and overseas, seeking out the big juicy finds, the newly discovered fields on other continents or out at sea - thus leaving behind tens of millions of barrels of oil for these small and mid-sized domestic producers to extract.

Domestic Oil Drilling Companies

Today, the U.S. Is home to hundreds of legitimate, small to mid-sized, family run oil drilling companies, many of whom have been in business for decades. These companies use continually improving technology, geological exploration techniques and equipment to uncover the most promising areas to drill new wells on already proven oil fields. There are many reasons why existing oil fields might continue to produce for decades, long after the big companies have moved on. For example, an old well might have been shut down during a prior downturn, never to be reopened for whatever reason, yet the oil remains there, underground, waiting to be harvested by a new operator.

A single well can cost anywhere from hundreds of thousands to millions of dollars. While big oil companies have access to billions of dollars in capital, a small company can quickly go bankrupt over a string of dry wells. While some of these family run companies have funds adequate to cover their drilling expenses, many others rely on a stable of long-standing associates who repeatedly pony up the necessary funds, while others venture out into the private sector to seek additional capital for drilling.

This fractured investment environment is not as straightforward as having your stockbroker go buy stock in an oil venture. Typically, direct oil and gas venture investments are found through word-of-mouth or web sites, with the investment made directly with the oil company, or sold through small brokers. In all cases, oil venture investing typically generates quite a bit of legal paperwork.

The good news is that federal and state agencies regulate this industry tightly, waging stiff penalties to those companies who do not follow oil industry regulations to the letter.

Exploratory vs Developmental Drilling

There are two types of oil drilling ventures, exploratory, or 'wildcat' drillers, and developmental drillers, with the latter being a far safer bet in that they drill in areas of known oil deposits. Exploratory drilling is more speculative and requires a far greater level of geological knowledge and funding, since wildcatters will tend to come across a lot more dry non-producing holes. Some oil drilling companies will engage in both types of drilling. For the novice oil ventures investor, the best type of company is, of course, the 'conservative' developmental drilling company, the one drilling low risk wells in areas of proven production.

The Revolution in Exploration

With the advent of 3-D seismic technologies in recent decades and other recent advances in technology and geological science, successfully finding oil in known fields has become a lot more dependable. The increase in quality a 3-D seismic analysis provides over the old 2-D technology is akin to a modern CAT scan vs an old x-ray. This 3-D revolution has given smaller independent oil companies the ability to compete with the majors, particularly on smaller leases. Using the new technologies, many oil drilling companies report success rates approaching 85% on exploratory wells and 95% on developmental wells. This, of course, benefits private and individual investors by giving them the ability to invest in oil and gas prospects previously considered the domain of the majors.

Types of Partnerships

Oil and gas investment types include limited partnerships, complex lease agreements, and general partnerships.

Limited partnerships involve the sale of partnership units to raise money for drilling activities. The sponsoring company charges a fee for managing the project and keeps a percentage of any revenue. Investors get a large first year tax write-off and quarterly cash distributions from any oil & gas found until the well runs dry.

General partnerships differ from limited partnerships in several key areas. General partners sometimes assist in the operations of the project. Second, they're personally responsible for debts incurred by the partnership.

Oil and gas drilling partnerships are difficult to turn quickly into cash and they generally have a relatively long holding period. This holding period is tempered by the fact that oil acts as a good long term hedge against oil price increases – which can act as a counterbalance to other investments in your portfolio. For instance, when stocks do badly, oil tends to do well.

Investor Requirements

While minimum investments in oil ventures are relatively low, generally tens of thousands of dollars, oil and gas companies prefer 'accredited investors'. An accredited investor is an individual or couple with a net worth of $1mil, not counting their primary residence, or with an annual income for the past two years of $200k for the individual or $300k for the couple.

Federal regulations do allow a certain number of non-accredited investors to participate in projects. Typically, non-accredited investors must show that they are sophisticated oil investors, having prior experience or education, and that they have a full understanding of the risks involved. Even non-accredited investors should be able to prove a net worth of $750,000. Regardless of this, non-accredited investors should limit their investment to a maximum of 20 percent of net worth.

Minimizing Risks

With proper due diligence and knowledge, there is no reason to expect that the average oil investor should not be able to see good, consistent year-over-year returns, ones rarely seen in other investment vehicles generally available to the private investor.

Besides, what investment today is risk-free? Even investments formerly considered 'safe' have demolished old verities and expectations. Stocks, formerly known for their annual returns of 10%-12%, have been all but flat over this past decade. Real estate has been a disaster, living and dying at the whims of the mortgage markets. Bonds and T-bills can no longer be counted on to provide decent returns.

An investor seeking to get into oil ventures can limit much of their risk through an understanding of what to look out for and what to avoid – in other words, through the study of the information contained in the remainder of this book, followed by further tutelage, preferably from an expert consultant, someone who already understands the industry. Once you have performed proper, informed due diligence on the company, the deal structure, and the geological reports, possibly with the assistance of said expert consultant, you should be well on your way to a good, promising deal.

1: Why oil is such a vital commodity

Oil and gas, more specifically natural gas, are 'sexy' - the perpetual darlings of the energy world. Despite intermittent chatter about other energy sources displacing oil's place at the top of the energy pyramid, the reality is that oil and, increasingly, natural gas are the two complementary energy sources located at the 'sweet spot' when it comes to their usefulness and value to the global economy. Relatively easy and inexpensive to acquire, process, transport, and use, with a high energy density per given amount of fuel, and an extensive, built-out infrastructure, oil and its myriad resultant products, is what runs modern global society.

Over the long term, oil is a finite and depleting commodity, not easily repleaceable. Many of the easy oil finds, the 'low hanging fruit', worldwide have been exploited. Yet, for every claim that 'peak oil' has been reached, the next year science keeps uncovering major new global finds, many of them not quite as easy to exploit, but that nontheless do exist under the ground. Indeed, the cursory layman's view would indicate that good portions of the world's continents are literally floating over vast deposits of oil and gas, and built atop beds of oil shale. The question, of course, becomes how easy is it to get at all this oil and gas?

Oil and natural gas are generally found together in nature, with many oil wells producing both oil and gas. Natural gas is the up and coming energy – largely due to its reputation as a cleaner, less polluting energy source that is more easily useable. But, because natural gas generally lies much deeper in the earth, it is considerably more difficult to get at than is oil, making oil a more valuable commodity than gas. That some oil wells offer up both oil and natural gas is a nice bonus for the lucky oil investor.

As a result of this decreasing reservoir of 'easy' oil, along with other political and environmental reasons, U.S. oil production has declined every year since 1971. Currently, we import 60% of our oil (twice the amount we imported before the oil embargo), much of it coming from countries that only intend ill will for America. Worse yet, our domestic oil stockpile is at a nearly three decade low.

And yet, global oil consumption shows no signs of easing, with T. Boone Pickens, billionaire oil investor, having last year predicted that we should expect $400 a barrel oil by 2020 (currently in the range of $80-100). Oil use has doubled over the past decade, and all indications are that oil use will double yet again during this decade. All this demand is reflected in the rise in the cost of a barrel of oil of over 300% since 2000 (in contrast to the stock markets, which have remained flat over this past decade).

For the private investor looking to place a toe into oil ventures, these are good times. The U.S. Government, through the use of unique tax breaks, is bending over backwards to encourage domestic oil ventures and reduce dependence on foreign oil imports.

In summary, oil is in as good a position as it has ever been. This is just a verity of life, without oil there is no modern world, try as we might like to wish it otherwise.

So, what other energy technologies might be waiting in the wings, to come into play in the coming decades? The following briefly summarizes the competing energy technologies and their shortcomings relative to oil/natural gas:

Competing Energy Technologies

Nuclear Fission

The unprecedented disaster at Fukashima has once again reminded us that nuclear energy, as currently developed, continues to be a supremely dangerous prospect, with Germany and other countries swearing off development of new reactors. There are several potentially novel nuclear technologies, requiring additional development before they can become feasible - including lithium based nuclear reactors that are safer and less polluting – but even if and when these designs were to come online, the timetables are decades long, with extensive deployment even further out into the future.

Coal

A technology older than oil, coal has always suffered from an image problem. It is considerably more polluting, requiring a lot more expensive mitigation technologies to make it cleaner, and it is more difficult than oil to extract and process. Coal certainly has its role in modern life, being one of the energy sources fueling China's economy, for instance (witness the nice clouds of pollution perpetually overhanging major Chinese cities), but it is no replacement for oil and likely will not be for a long time, if ever.

Biofuels

A more recent newcomer to the world of energy, biofuels have a relatively bright future, with genetic engineering allowing for development of new plants that produce ever larger energy yields per acre. Alas, all this promise is largely dashed when one realizes the tremendous amount of land and resources required to grow the immense volumes of plant material required for biomass to have practical use as an energy source. As the world's arable land resources continue to be strained by the need to feed an ever burgeoning populace, the equations, both in terms of dollars and in terms of priorities, just do not work out.

Solar

An evergreen technology, solar has long been saddled with low energy yield results, meaning given a square yard of solar panel, only so much energy can today be extracted practically. On the other hand, solar is one of those technologies that, barring a few major materials science breakthroughs, where solar cell efficacy might be increased 3 or 4 fold, there is still potential for solar to become a significant player in the coming decades. Even granting this, solar is practical only in certain applications, such as helping light and cool buildings, but is all but useless when dealing with vehicles or in manufacturing, except under limited circumstances.

Wind

Another perpetual contender to chip away at oil's dominance, wind has some rather major tradeoffs. While the energy extracted from the wind is essentially free, once the wind tower has been installed, there are limits to where this technology is practical, with only certain regions and zones of the world having sufficient, consistently high wind speeds to make wind energy a practical, large scale reality. Add in the NIMBY (not in my backyard) crowd, and the often vast distances between windy regions and the large population centers that need the energy, and the picture is considerably less rosy.

Geothermal

A good, efficient, 'green' source of energy, geothermal is only practical in certain areas of the world.

Water Power

Many of the prime waterway locations for dams worldwide have already been exploited.

Nuclear Fusion

Perpetually 20 years from practical deployment, fusion energy is one of those elusive technologies that always manages to remain ahead of the scientists' grasps. Were fusion to even make a major breakthrough in the next decade, testing, developing, then ramping up the technology would still take decades before it began to substantively displace existing energy technologies.

Other, more esoteric technologies

Such as cold fusion, zero point energy, etc... – While there continue to be murmurs of breakthroughs in such technologies, the prognosis so far is that if and when these scientific conceits were ever to become more than fantasy or conjecture or theory, any sea change in energy use will take decades to occur, and anyway, oil is and for a long time will continue to be the go-to energy source, both from a standpoint of ease of acquisition and production to convenience of use to energy density per given quantity of fuel.

Certainly, there is always the chance the next decade may bring a slew of cross-industry breakthroughs, in materials science, in physics theories, in genetics that, coupled together, might manage to bang out a budding new practical energy economy, but the current reality is that oil continues to be cheap and easy, relatively speaking, which is why the world continues to depend on oil as its mainstay.

The United States government understands the critical importance of oil, so much so that the IRS has long deployed a series of unique tax breaks and benefits, unavailable to any other industry, to those willing to invest money into oil drilling and production.

2: Summary of domestic oil industry

The oil industry is composed of many different scales and levels of involvement. The oil giants - Exxon, Chevron, BP - are some of the biggest and wealthiest corporations on the planet, investing hundreds of billions globally in the hopes of uncovering the next great oil region. Meanwhile, a smaller but equally lucrative marketplace exists, where small and mid-sized family run oil drilling companies make their living, finding and exploring smaller fields or using newer technologies to extract additional oil from existing, already proven fields.

In the United States particularly, many of the big easy finds have been exploited by the majors, leaving those companies to go offshore and to other continents. But domestically, many extant fields remain quite healthy and poised to continue quietly producing millions of barrels a day for decades to come. One advantage of local American oil production is that it continues to reduce our country's dependence on foreign oil, a big reason the US government maintains the many enormous and unique tax benefits available only to those drilling for oil.

As a result of America's desire to stimulate domestic oil production, investment in oil ventures remain the last legal tax 'shelter' [of a sort] in the U.S., offering many tax deductions and write offs unique to the industry. The following is a brief synopsis of the domestic oil ventures industry.

Exploratory vs Developmental Drilling

Exploratory drilling, also called 'wild-catting', is used primarily to search for oil in areas with potentially astronomical stakes but with no prior oil excavations. If a new oil field is found, considerable profits can be made, but a run of dry holes can wipe out an investor. Ongoing advances in exploration and drilling technology are continually reducing the risks of exploratory drilling. Exploratory drilling does pose more risk than developmental drilling as there is never any certainty of an oil strike. As a result, many wells may need to be sunk before an oil bed is actually found.

Developmental Drilling is primarily done in areas with previously discovered oil beds. Conservative companies tend to use this method as it is more likely to strike oil or gas. With recent advances in drilling, new wells can often be sunk profitably, using the latest equipment, right next to old, low production wells. A well may even be re-drilled down the same old well hole if research shows that there may still be substantial oil at that location.

Oil drilling is an expensive proposition, with a single well costing anywhere from hundreds of thousands to millions of dollars. As a result, oil drilling companies regularly seek capital in order to construct new wells on proven fields or to rework outdated units.

Though developmental drilling companies may pose a safer bet, there are still many financial risks involved in this type of investment. For this reason, only accredited investors are legally able to invest in oil and gas ventures.

Drilling Procedures

An oil company deciding to drill at a certain location first makes sure all lease agreements and right of ways are completed. They then clear and level the land for drilling, building access roads and digging pits for the rigs. Oil and gas well drilling rigs are then brought in. Drilling crews drill a hole to a pre-set depth, above the estimated location of the oil or gas. They then put casing pipe into the hole and a cement crew pumps cement down the pipe. The cement is tested for hardness and checked for a proper seal. This process is then continued until the well reaches its final depth. Once the final depth is reached, oil is allowed to flow into the casing in a controlled manner. If oil initially fails to flow, numerous methods can be used to get the oil moving, depending on type of well and situation.

Advances in Exploration Technology

Since the mid 1990s the industry has enjoyed technological breakthroughs in 3-D seismic surveys that allow much more accurate identification of accumulations of oil and gas. 3-D versus 2-D is like looking at a CAT scan versus a regular x-ray. The 3-D revolution has given smaller independent oil companies the ability to compete with the majors, particularly on smaller leases. In turn, this benefits private capital and the individual investor, by affording the ability to invest in oil and gas prospects, previously considered the domain of the majors.

Types Of Ownership

A limited partner is one whose risk is limited to the capital contribution made. In any loss, the limited partner's capital contribution covers the risk involved. The limited partner enjoys tax breaks, depreciation deductions, and oil depletion allowances.

A general partner assumes all risk other than the capital put up by the limited partners. Benefits enjoyed are similar to those enjoyed by limited partners. The general partner manages the venture.

Rather than merely investing in oil stocks or futures, becoming a limited partner, also referred to as a direct partnership program (DPP), allows one to enjoy significant IRS tax breaks and potentially high profits without having to take on the full burden, risk and responsibility of owning an oil and gas exploration company.

There are several ways one can get involved with an oil drilling company. The company can either sell direct limited partnerships, or an investor can go through a broker-dealer. The broker-dealer is responsible for completing due diligence on projects: that the company truly does own the leases, has authority to sell the project, the geology makes sense, and the project is properly put together. Registered broker-dealers are required to send out a Private Placement Memorandum (PPM) which includes details on the project and deal. The potential investor needs to know how to break down the numbers in a PPM in order to determine how much oil or gas needs to be produced to break even.

Accredited Investor

Not just anyone can invest in limited partnerships. The US government requires one investing in oil and gas to be an Accredited Investor, namely:

• A director, executive officer, or general partner of the issuer of securities.

- Any natural individual whose net worth exceeds $1,000,000, either individually or as a couple, excluding the primary residence.
- Any natural person with income exceeding $200,000 in each of the last 2 years, or a couple with income exceeding $300,000, with the expectation of similar income in the coming year.
- Any trust or organization with more than $5million in assets that was not formed solely with the purpose of acquiring securities
- Any entity where all equity owners are accredited investors.

3: Oil Ventures – Benefits and Rewards

Many of the largest, most profitable global corporations are oil companies, for a wealth of reasons. Oil ventures allow even smaller private investors willing to invest as little as $50k to enjoy the ample profits and extensive, unique tax benefits available to the giants.

Quick Initial Payback

Return on initial capital in as little as 6 to 18 months.

Generally, monthly revenue checks should begin to come in within 60 to 90 days after a well starts to produce gas or oil.

Long Term Value

Contrary to expectations, oil and gas properties actually increase in value with age. This is because fields originally bypassed can be accessed later, using newer techniques and equipment that leads to better extraction.

Ongoing cash flow from a successful well can last more than a decade

Big Upside Potential

If the first well in a new field is a success, all subsequent wells are much lower risk pure profit plays.

Established, Liquid Market

Oil and gas property auctions have flourished, making the buying and selling of anything from fractional wells to multiple wells, including royalties, overriding royalties and working interests, that much easier.

Stable & Safe Investment

Owning an oil investment protects you against fluctuations in the oil market.

Oil investments respond inversely to most markets, allowing you to balance your portfolio.

Owning oil is a hedge against future oil price increases.

Oil is a vital asset – first and second world countries live and die by their ability to access or purchase oil.

Protected Asset

Oil, being underground, cannot be destroyed in time of war or natural disaster and is protected from theft.

Increasing Market Demand Coupled With Decreasing Supply

Oil and gas prices increase over time. Billionaire oil investor T. Boone Pickens predicts $400 a barrel oil by 2020.

Petroleum demand doubles every 10 years., the primary markets being China, India, and the U.S.

U.S. stockpiles are at a 30 year low.

Imports are now over 60% (they were 30% prior to the the Arab oil embargo).

Oil and gas prices are up over 300% since 2000. (stock markets have essentially been flat this past decade)

Decreasing Risk Profile

With emerging exploration technologies coming online all the time, many companies currently report a success rate of 85% on exploratory wells and 95% on developmental wells.

Lucrative

Greater than 50% annual rate of return is possible.

Long term returns of 5:1 to 10:1 on initial investment are common.

Considerable Tax Benefits

The U.S. is heavily invested in seeking to stimulate domestic oil production

Oil ventures are the last legal tax 'shelter' in the US, offering numerous tax deductions and write offs.

Investors can write off nearly the entire investment.

An inflation hedge, oil is the only tax investment still available to individuals that is protected no matter which way the economy moves.

OIL VENTURES 101

The generous tax benefits offered to oil ventures are found nowhere else in the tax code - allowing you to offset other sources of income.

Many experienced oil and gas investors permanently avoid federal income tax altogether by "reinvesting" their oil and gas income - that is, they continually reinvest their money in new oil and natural gas projects. In this way, they get a compounded growth on their oil and gas income in the ground, tax-free forever. Few independent oil companies ever pay much income tax.

Intangible drilling costs, which go toward labor and other unrecoverable costs, usually make up about 40% to 80% of the investment and can be written off in the first year.

The remaining 20% to 60% is typically written off over time, using either a straight-line depreciation over seven years, or over the expected life of the well.

If the well is a dry hole, the entire investment can be written off.

In some cases, tax incentives can reduce an investor's tax bracket.

The write-off can be as much as 35% or more against your adjusted gross income.

These breaks offer a sizeable risk hedge, where the worst case scenario is a 65% loss on the initial investment, provided there are no additional capital calls and the investor is in the 35% tax bracket.

Tax Breaks In Detail

The intangible drilling costs can be 40-80% of the cost of drilling a well. These costs are 100% tax deductible - geological studies, exploration, rental of the drilling rig, wages, fuel, supply costs - these expenses can be deducted in a single year or amortized over 60 months. (IRC 263(c) and 59(e) treasury regulations 1.612 parts 4 and 5)

Depreciation

Materials and equipment over a 7 year period, either accelerated or straight line. (IRC (b) and (c))

Tangible completion expenses

20-60% of the total cost of operating the well.

Depletion allowance

15-20% of gross annual revenue is exempt from taxes. (IRC sec 611, 613, 613A(c)(6))

Geological deductions

This is a more recent deduction associated with the development of the well, deductible over a 24 month period. (IRC 167(h))

Self-employment tax, and conversion from a general partner to a limited partner

A general partner's share of net income or loss constitutes earnings from self-employment. It is likely there will be a loss in the year the well was drilled (due to IDC). This loss may be used to offset self-employment income. Generally, after a general partner converts to a limited partner, income from the partnership is not subject to self-employment tax. Because the partnership carries no debt, a general partner's conversion to limited partner status should not result in adverse tax consequences. (IRC 1402, Rev. Rul. 84-52, 1984 -1 C.B. 157).

Alternative minimum tax

Depletion allowance has been repealed as a tax preference item, reduction in AMT up to 40% of excess intangible drilling costs. (IRC 57(a)(2)(E))

Passive activity exception

Working interests in oil and gas property are exempt from being defined as passive activity. (IRC 469(c)(3)(A)). Because general partners' initial losses are not passive, all income from the well is treated as non-passive (IRC 469(c)(3)(B))

Special rule for timing of deductions

Investors in oil and gas partnerships are allowed to deduct the expenses for drilling in the year the investment was made if paid by December 31. Drilling operations must begin within

90 days of the end of the partnership's established tax year. (IRC 461(i)(2)(A)).

Marginal well production credits

When the published IRS reference price is less than a bench marked price point , additional tax credits (up to 50 cents per mcf or $3 per barrel) may be available to the investor in a gas and oil partnership. (IRC 38 and 45I).

This information is not to be used for tax advice. As with all investments, investors are urged to consult with their attorney or tax advisor as to the benefits of oil and gas investment with regard to federal income tax consequences and how it applies to individual tax situations.

4: OIL VENTURES – RISKS AND HOW TO AVOID THEM

Risk: Dry Hole

Hitting a dry hole is an obvious systemic risk in any oil and gas investing, no matter how otherwise legitimate a company may be.

How To Minimize The Risk Of Dry Holes

To avoid the risk of dry holes, one can buy into already producing wells, in which case the biggest risk becomes the depletion curve (when the oil runs out), and any costs to keep the oil going.

In order to mitigate risks, one can invest a portion of their investment funds in multiple oil projects, that way, if one well fails, the other wells can make up for any loss.

Risk: Bad Companies

Inexperienced Drilling Companies

In their eagerness to enhance returns, some companies may accidentally damage or destroy the structure of the well. 'Overstimulation', as it is called, can destroy a well.

SEE BELOW FOR REMEDIES

Unscrupulous Companies

Many companies out there can talk a great game, but they are not properly licensed with the NASD or SEC.

A company might lie and say the well hit, then request more funds to cover costs, during which they may even send out a check or two as 'evidence' that the well hit. But that amounts to nothing more than a Ponzi scheme, as the money may very well be taken from the investor's original funds.

Some drilling companies may drill multiple holes in an area, hit one big well, and then state that that was their own well, but that this dry hole over here is the one that you were invested in.

SEE BELOW FOR REMEDIES

Scam Artists

The biggest risk for investors is to make sure the company is legitimate. One tried and true technique scam artists use is to set up the company (limited liability company or corporation) in one state, drill in another state, and sell shares to investors in every state but those two. This reduces the likelihood an investor will drop by and discover the company has neither offices nor drilling fields.

Scam artists typically engage in use of telemarketing boiler rooms and/or email promotions (spam) to find dupes. Run the other way whenever you encounter any promises of 'guaranteed' returns or 'can't miss' claims or if you are not given a chance to look over materials. Any of the following 'pressure' techniques are a giveaway:

"There's no risk in this investment.."

"This well is guaranteed to make money."

"...A geologist gave me this tip."

"There has been a huge "discovery" in an adjoining field."

"A well known oil company is planning to drill in the area."

"This deal is open to only a few, unique investors, such as yourself."

"...Only a few shares left. To get in on this, you need to send us money right away."

"This is one investment that just can't miss..."

"Profitibility isn't even in question..."

"You'll make a lot of money."

Look out for companies overselling a project, making it sound too good to be true.

If somebody says they've already drilled the well, and they just need you to pay some money to complete the well in exchange for an interest, that is usually an indication of a scam.

Staff at these places typically know little about the oil business.

They may send you expensive looking professional brochures, but savvy investors know never to invest based only on a phone call and glossy brochure.

How To Minimize Risk of Getting Involved With Inexperienced, Unscrupulous, Or Scam Companies

The following comprehensive checklist is an assemblage of advice from a number of sources including state regulators and experts in the oil ventures field. You should have answers to all of the questions regarding 1.) the company involved 2.) the structure of the deal and 3.) the geology of the site - available to you prior to putting a penny into any oil venture.

In summary:

• Is the company and its principals/partners established, knowledgeable, properly registered, forthcoming, transparent, and available to speak with you?

• Are they proper documents, registered with the state, clear and complete, with information about the specific oil well being drilled?

• Is the salesperson or broker knowledgeable, forthcoming and transparent about their arrangement with the operator?

• Is the type and quality of the deal worth your time, money and effort?

To get the proper due diligence information pulled together takes a substantial amount of time and effort. State securities regulators advise potential investors to never be afraid to ask the tough questions. Prior to investing, always run the name of a company and/or broker by your state securities administrator. They have information on operators, legitimate and not, and are there to protect investors from fraud (www.nasaa.org). Also, seek out the advice and guidance of a neutral expert consultant before committing any funds. Your best bet is to always choose well established, long running, experienced oil exploration and production companies.

The following is a detailed breakdown of all the questions to which you will need to know the answers:

Is The Company And The Offering Properly Registered?

Registered firms are regularly audited by the SEC, NASD and state securities boards, and have to follow a complete disclosure requirement. Thus, any legitimate company will be registered with some [but not necessarily all] of the following agencies: The NASD (National Association of Securities Dealers), SEC (Securities and Exchange Commission), FINRA (Financial Industry Regulatory Authority), the security board of the state in which the company is doing business. They should also have a D&B (Dun & Bradstreet) number and/or easily available financials.

Is the offering filed with the state securities commission in your state or where the company is located? Contact that agency to find out more about the company and the offering.

If the company claims exemption from registration requirements in the state where the offer or sale is being made, ask them which exemption and the terms of that exemption. Contact the state securities agency to confirm the offering is indeed exempt.

If the company claims a security is not involved at all, find out why, then contact the state securities agency to confirm whether what is being offered really is a security or not.

Is The Company Established And Does It Have A Good Track Record?

• Invest only with companies having a substantial track record in the business.

• Ask for names of company principals and general partners, along with their background and experience in oil and gas drilling operations and their history with the company.

• Find out the company's oil drilling operations history, including the number of wells drilled and/or completed as producing wells, and whether the company retained its interests in the drilled wells.

• Find out the company's capitalization, assets and retained earnings. Does it have sufficient funds to cover unexpected costs?

• What is the name and address of the operator and their experience with ventures of this nature? What are the terms of the agreement with the operator, including the compensation terms?

Is Company Information Readily Available Publicly?

• Research and investigation into a company and its track record ought to be relatively straightforward. If getting at a company's information is difficult, that is a sign that the company may not be legitimate.

Is The Company Being Forthcoming And Not Hesitating To Provide You With Information?

- You should be able to easily obtain information on who the principals and general partners of the company are, what experience they bring, and what kind of funds the company has to cover the costs involved, among other information.

Are The Principals Generally Available?

- Always demand an opportunity to speak with one of the principals/partners.

Is The Company Willing To Put Everything In Writing?

- Ask for everything in writing and demand full disclosure.

Is The Salesperson Legitimate, Knowledgeable And Forthcoming?

- Ask for the name of the person offering the security. Ask about their background in oil or gas ventures and where they are calling from.

- The salesperson ought to be eager to freely volunteer written and oral explanations to questions.

- Contact your state securities agency to find out if the salesperson has been sanctioned for previous violations of securities law

There are specific licensing requirements for those selling partnerships and other investments in oil and gas options. Ask about the company and the commission structure. Ask the salesperson what commission or compensation they will get. Determine if conflicts of interest involving the promoter are disclosed. Insist on seeing a copy of the operator's contract with the promoter.

Are You Being Given The Proper Legal Paperwork? Is It Properly Prepared?

• Registered broker-dealers are required to send out a Private Placement Memorandum (PPM), a prospectus or offering document which includes all the information on a company, its principals, its history and track record, and revenues that the promoter must furnish to potential investors before they commit any funds.

Is The Company Properly Handling Your Funds?

• Make sure funds are kept in a separate escrow account and not commingled with other funds. Make sure the funds will not be used for purposes other than those specified. Get these things in writing.

• Ask what type of conveyance document will be provided after any investment is made.

Have The Total Costs Of The Venture Been Disclosed?

• Ask what the total well completion costs will be for each investor, including additional commissions to be paid, and whether investors are obligated to pay in more money in the future.

• Ask how much money they seek to raise and the cost per fractional interest. Ask how much they intend to spend on ads, salaries, sales commissions, and estimated profits to the company.

- Ask about intangible drilling costs.

- Ask about tax incentives available in the event of a dry-hole.

Have You Been Given Specifics On The Precise Location Of The Drilling Operation?

- Get a legal description of the property to be drilled on, specifically indicating the precise well location where the operator plans to drill.

- Secure a statement of the depth of the well to be drilled and an indication of when drilling is to begin.

Have You Been Given Specifics About The Nature Of The Lease Deal?

- How and when was this lease acquired? Is the lease being sold to the venture at cost. If not, how much profit is being made?

- Find out if the lease is already in default and whether there is any overriding royalty or landowner's royalty or other leasehold burden being paid.

- Ask for a disclosure of the person selling the lease, the cost of the lease and any relationship between the lessor and the operator.

- You should be suspicious of any limited liability company that is being formed solely for the purpose of the specific investment offering.

- Consider obtaining insurance to protect yourself.

Does The Company Have Major Existing Liabilities?

• Does the company have contingent liabilities from other ventures?

Are You Dealing With The Proper Legal Entity?

• It is preferable for you to invest with the operator doing the actual drilling.

• You should be receiving revenue directly from the purchaser, not the operator.

Does The Company Or Salesperson Use Pressure Tactics On You?

• Resist pressure to make hurried, uninformed investment decisions.

Are You Capable Of Analyzing In Detail The Paperwork Being Given You?

Hopefully, you find this book to be of value to you in gaining a basic picture of this business (if so, let others know about us). But this book is only the initial step. A potential investor needs to know how to analyze the numbers in a PPM in order to determine how much oil or gas needs to be produced for them to break even. If you do not know the answers to questions, ask for assistance or advice from someone who does know.

Do The Geology, Type Of Well And Financials Make Sense?

• Is this a 'wildcat' or exploratory well or is it a developmental well?

• Is this well in an area of proven oil reserves, with relatively successful nearby wells, offering good yields? Ask for details about nearby properties, including local well completions and a geologist's report on the area.

• Make certain the net revenue interest is less than 70% of the working interest

Can You Seek Out Someone To Help You Negotiate A Deal?

• Ask among your peers for recommendations and references. Seek advice from others who know the business and are willing to educate you about it.

• An assignment deed is preferable.

• Get them to give you an AFE (Approval For Expenditure) which outlines the actual costs of the deal.

Do You Have Answers To The Following Questions?

• Who is responsible for payment of taxes? Will they be paid out of the investor's share?

• Is the tax treatment of the investments, as claimed by the company, supported by the IRS?

- What is the location of available pipelines, or what method will be used to transport and sell any production?

- How will the decision be made for completing the well or abandoning it? Who will make that decision?

- What is to become of funds received from the salvage value of equipment on the lease?

Conclusion

Given that all of these questions are answered to your satisfaction, you should have a clear path to a legitimate, fair, and fruitful oil venture.

ETC.

Consult With Legitimate Oil Venture Firms

A primary service of **OilVentures101.org** is to act as a safe conduit between you, the accredited investor, and legitimate Better Business Bureau rated and accredited small-to-mid-sized oil venture companies, many of whom are family run operations in the oil venture business for decades, yet with scant resources to find legitimate investors on their own.

If you are genuinely interested in oil ventures, I strongly encourage you to visit the OilVentures101.org web site and fill out the form on the left hand column with your contact information, at which point one or several oil venture partners would contact you to answer any outstanding questions.

General Inquiries/Comments

Send *comments, concerns, critiques, thank-you notes, recommendations, reviews, corrections, information, updates, media inquiries,* or anything else:

- **OilVentures101@gmail.com**

Also, visit my web site periodically for book updates, discussions, blogs, articles, or to post a note via the contact page.

- **www.OilVentures101.org**

...If you don't like something you see here, tell me. If you do like something, <u>tell others</u>.

ABOUT the Author

Robert Wellesley is founder of Oil Ventures 101 [OilVentures101.org] and is a graduate of the MBA program at the University of Texas and the Pratt Institute in New York City.

Robert is also the founder of Sequence Marketing & Publishing. Robert lives in Austin, Texas.

ABOUT OilVentures101.org

Oil ventures are among the oldest, most stable and lucrative investment vehicles available to the individual investor, one offering unrivaled tax benefits.

Oil Ventures 101 was established by a team of seasoned oil venture experts with the goal of becoming the single most trusted, reliable and objective information resource in this growing and profitable sector.

Additionally, our organization seeks to act as a conduit for the industry, giving accredited investors the opportunity to gather more specific information by consulting directly with our top Better Business Bureau rated and accredited small-to-mid-sized oil venture companies, many of whom are family run operations that have been in the oil venture business for decades.

www.ingramcontent.com/pod-product-compliance
Lightning Source LLC
Chambersburg PA
CBHW071820170526
45167CB00003B/1386